Songbook Edition

PICK a PACK
50 SONGS OF FUN of AND FAITH FOR KIDS
PRAISE

ARRANGED BY
JOSEPH LINN

COMPILED BY KEN BIBLE

ADVISORY COMMITTEE
LYNDELL LEATHERMAN · WILMA WILSON · JOSEPH AND ROZANNE LINN

A SEQUEL TO
SING A SONG OF SCRIPTURE

PUBLISHING COMPANY

KANSAS CITY, MO 64141

Abundawonderful Medley

Arr. by Joseph Linn

I HEARD ABOUT: vv. 1 & 2, medley ending 2nd time. "ABUNDAWONDERFUL" LIFE IN JESUS: vv. 1 & 2, medley ending 2nd time.

1   I Heard About

(Gen. 8:4; Josh. 6; 10:12-13; Judg. 16:22; 1 Sam. 17:40; Ezek. 37:1-10; Dan. 6:16-22; Jon.)

R. C.

RALPH CARMICHAEL

1. I heard a-
2. I heard a-

bout old No - ah   land - in' on the moun - tain
bout old Josh - ua   tear - in' down old Jer - i -

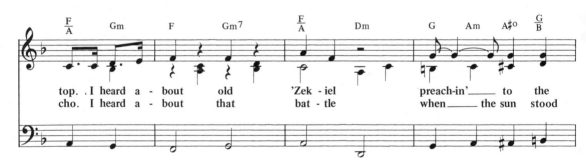

top. I heard a - bout old 'Zek - iel preach-in'____ to the
cho. I heard a - bout that bat - tle when____ the sun stood

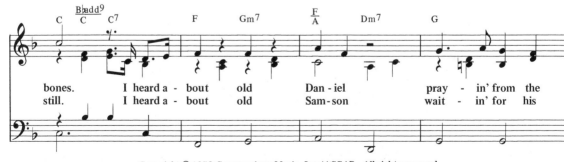

bones. I heard a - bout old Dan - iel pray - in' from the
still. I heard a - bout old Sam - son wait - in' for his

2   "Abundawonderful" Life in Jesus

(John 10:10)

K. H.

KATHIE HILL

Steadfast Medley

Arr. by Joseph Linn

MY HEART IS STEADFAST: four times, medley ending 4th time. YES, LORD, YES: twice, medley ending 2nd time.

3 My Heart Is Steadfast

(Ps. 16:8; 57:7)

B. C. and E. K.

BRIAN CARR and ED KEE

My heart ___ is stead - fast; ___ What He does in me ___ will last. ___

4

Yes, Lord, Yes

L. K.

(Matt. 6:10)

LYNN KEESECKER

Yes, Lord, yes! to Your will and to Your way.

5

All We Like Sheep

(Isa. 53:6; John 10:11; 14:15; 1 Pet. 2:21)

K. H.

KATHIE HILL

1. Each lamb is pre - cious to
2. God proved His love for us

Je - sus, our Shep-herd; We can't wan-der out of His love.
when He sent Je - sus To show us the way we should live.

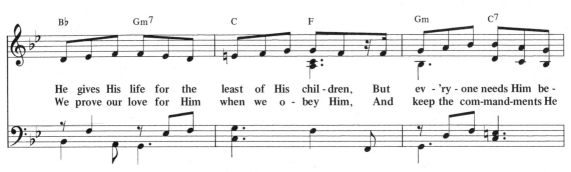

He gives His life for the least of His chil - dren, But ev - 'ry - one needs Him be-
We prove our love for Him when we o - bey Him, And keep the com-mand-ments He

cause
gives.

All we like sheep have gone a - stray.

Everything Is His Medley

Arr. by Joseph Linn

ALL THINGS BRIGHT AND BEAUTIFUL: once. EVERYTHING THAT IS, IS HIS: cho., v. 1; cho., v. 2; coda.

6 All Things Bright and Beautiful

(Gen. 1)

CECIL G. ALEXANDER

BURYL RED

All things bright and beau - ti - ful, All things great and small,

All things wise and won - der - ful; Our Fa - ther made them all.

Cold winds in win - ter, Pleas - ant sum - mer sun,

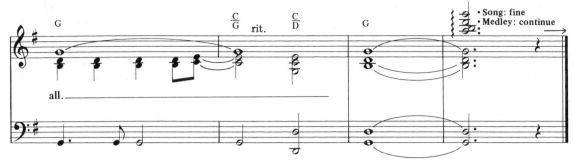

7

Everything That Is, Is His

KATHIE HILL

(1 Chron. 29:14; Ps. 24:1-2)

DAVID HAMPTON

Ev-'ry-thing that is, is His; All that's un-der and be-side us, the Fa-ther has sup-plied us. God's still the own-er; He's just loan-ing it, you see, 'Cause ev-'ry-thing that is, is His!

Alphabet Medley

Arr. by Joseph Linn

A-B-C-D-E-F-G: once, medley transition. I AM A "C": twice, medley ending 2nd time.

8

A-B-C-D-E-F-G

(John 3:16)

HUGH MITCHELL

H. M.

A - B - C - D -

E - F - G, Je - sus died for you and me.

H - I - J - K - L - M - N, Je - sus died for sin - ful

men. A - men! O - P - Q - R - S - T - U,

I be - lieve God's Word is true. U - V -

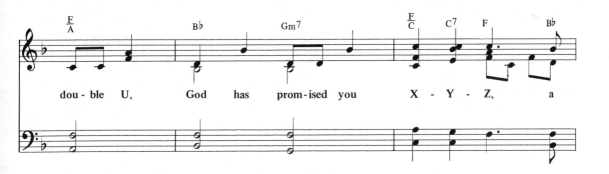

dou - ble U, God has prom-ised you X - Y - Z, a

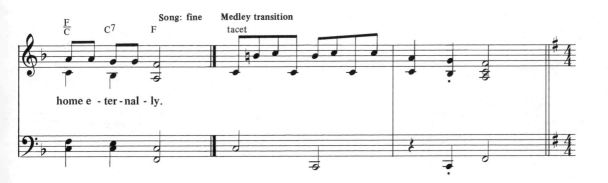

Song: fine   Medley transition
             tacet

home e - ter - nal - ly.

9

Traditional

I Am a "C"

(Acts 11:26; Gal. 2:20)

Traditional
Arr. by Joseph Linn

I am a

Jesus Medley

Arr. by Joseph —

LET'S TALK ABOUT JESUS: twice, medley ending 2nd time. HIS NAME IS LIFE: once.

10 Let's Talk About Jesus

(John 8:58; 10:9; 14:6; Rev. 19:16)

Traditional

Traditional
Arr. by Joseph Linn

Let's talk a-bout Je - sus, the King of Kings is He, The Lord of Lords su - preme through all e - ter - ni - ty; The great I

AM, the Way, the Truth, the Life, the Door.

Let's talk a - bout Je - sus more and

Song ending
F

(D.S.)

Medley ending
F

more.

more.

11 His Name Is Life

(Ps. 18:2; Isa. 9:6; Matt. 21:9; John 1:36-38; 4:42; 10:11; 14:6; 1 Cor. 2:8; Rev. 5:5; 15:3)

C. L.

CARMAN LICCIARDELLO and WILLIAM J. GAITHER

His name is Mas - ter,

Sav - ior, Li - on of Ju - dah, Bless - ed Prince of____

12

Jesus Loves
(Matt. 19:14)

Anon.
Adapted by J. F.

JILL FREEMAN
Arr. by Joseph Linn

13 Love Is the Greatest Gift of All

(1 Cor. 13)

P. J. and H. J.

PETER and HANNEKE JACOBS

1. If I could speak like an an - gel,_____ Or know what to - mor - row may bring;
2. God's love is nev - er de - mand - ing,_____ But al - ways is gen - tle and kind.

If I had faith to move moun - tains,_____ That would-n't mean a
God's love is al - ways for - giv - ing,_____ Leav-ing the past be -

Sing a Song Medley

Arr. by Joseph Linn

IF YOU CAN SING A SONG: vv. 1-3. I WILL SING, I WILL SING: vv. 1 & 2, medley ending 2nd time.

14   If You Can Sing a Song

(Ps. 146:2)

P. J. and H. J.

PETER and HANNEKE JACOBS

With a shuffle

1. 3. If you can sing a song, then praise the Lord.
2. If you can reach up high, then praise the Lord.

If you can hum a-long, then praise the Lord. If you can sit down
And try to touch the sky, then praise the Lord. Just like the green leaves

on the ground, turn your bod-y all a-round, or make a hap-py sound, praise the
on the tree sway-in' in the sum-mer breeze make a mel-o-dy to the

15

I Will Sing, I Will Sing

(Ps. 146:1-2)

MAX DYER

16 A Great Big God

(Gen. 1; Isa. 66:2)

M. P.

MARK PENDERGRASS

1. You hung all the stars and named them one by one; You rolled out the moon and lit the sun. Tip-ping up the moun-tains, pour-ing out the sea; Then You turned a-round and You made me. You're a

2. You con-trol the thun-der, cause the wind to blow, Send the driv-ing rain and si-lent snow; O-pen ev-'ry flow-er, col-or ev-'ry tree; Then You sit right down and talk to me. You're a

REFRAIN

17 Zeroes into Heroes

(Judg. 6-7)

JOANNE BARRETT and D. T.

DWIGHT THOMAS
Arr. by Joseph Linn

*1. God can take those ze-roes And turn them in - to he - roes.
2. God can take your trou-bles And pop them like they're bub-bles.
*3. When you feel like noth-ing And you've lost all your stuff-ing,

He did it all through his - to - ry;___ He can do it a - gain to - day.
He did it all through his - to - ry;___ He can do it a - gain to - day.
Re - mem-ber God is still num-ber one.___ Is He your num - ber one to - day?

He'll take your fear and doubt-ing And
And when your faith is sag - ging, And He'll
For when He stands be - side you And

Everybody Praise Medley

Arr. by Joseph Linn

DOXOLOGY: once, medley ending. CREATURE PRAISE: vv. 1-3, with refrain; medley ending 3rd time.

18 Doxology
(Ps. 103:20-22)

THOMAS KEN

JIMMY OWENS

Praise God,_____ from_____ whom all bless - ings flow.

Praise Him, _____ all crea - tures here_____ be -

19 Creature Praise

(Ps. 148:7, 10; 150:6)

DAVID MATTHEWS

Lyrics:

1. Large creatures, small creatures, short and tall creatures,
2. Low creatures, high creatures, flyin' in the sky creatures, Come now and praise the Lord.
3. Day creatures, night creatures, left and right creatures,

Young creatures, old creatures, hot and cold creatures,
White creatures, brown creatures, all the world around creatures,
Near creatures, far creatures, anywhere you are creatures,

Come now and praise the Lord.

REFRAIN

Sing praise to the Father, sing praise to the Son, Sing praise to the Spirit who

20
All Night, All Day
(Ps. 91:11-12)

Spiritual

Spiritual
Arr. by Joseph Linn

With a shuffle

*1. Day is dy - in' in the
2. Now I lay me down to
love stay with me through the

west;
sleep;
night;

An - gels watch-in' o - ver me, my Lord. I
And

Sleep, my child, and take your rest;
pray the Lord my soul to keep;
wake me with the morn - ing light;

*Verses 1 & 3 on recording.

REFRAIN

21

I'm Gonna Hide God's Word Inside My Heart

(Ps. 119:11)

P. J. and H. J.

PETER and HANNEKE JACOBS

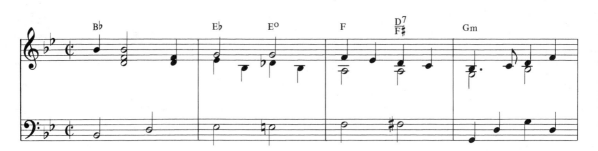

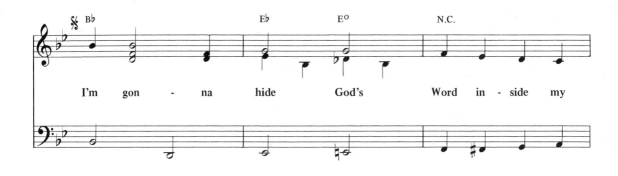

I'm gon - na hide God's Word in - side my

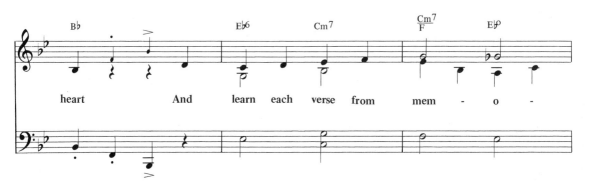

heart And learn each verse from mem - o -

22

Roots
(Ps. 1:1-3)

RICK POWELL

R. P.

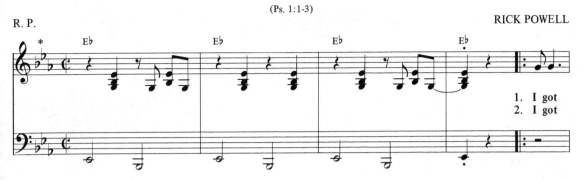

1. I got
2. I got

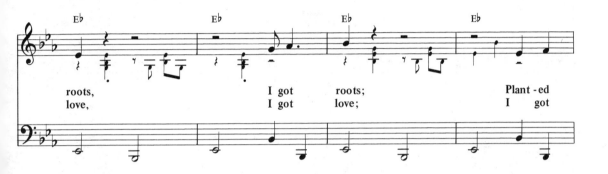

roots,   I got roots;   Plant-ed
love,   I got love;   I got

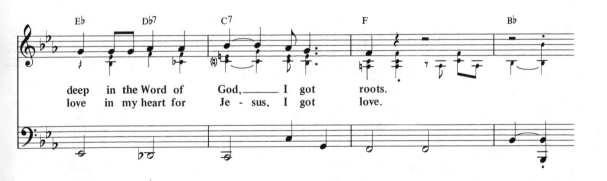

deep in the Word of God,___ I got roots.
love in my heart for Je - sus, I got love.

I got roots,   I got roots;
I got love,   I got love;

*The recording and trax for this song are in the key of F.

Jesus, I Love You Medley

Arr. by Joseph Linn

GIFTS IN MY HEART: vv. 1 & 2, medley ending 2nd time. JESUS, I LOVE YOU: vv. 1 & 3, medley ending 2nd time.

23

Gifts in My Heart

(Ps. 116:12-14)

BETSY HERNANDEZ

B. H.

1. There are gifts in my heart, And I
2. More than dia - monds or gold Are the
3. Though He owns all the stars, All the

give them to the Lord Ev - 'ry time that I sing
gifts that my heart holds, And my song is the key
world and all there is, What He cher - ish - es most

Songs of prais - es to my King._____
That un - locks and sets them free._____
Are the gifts His chil - dren give._____

© 1985 Garden Valley Music (ASCAP).

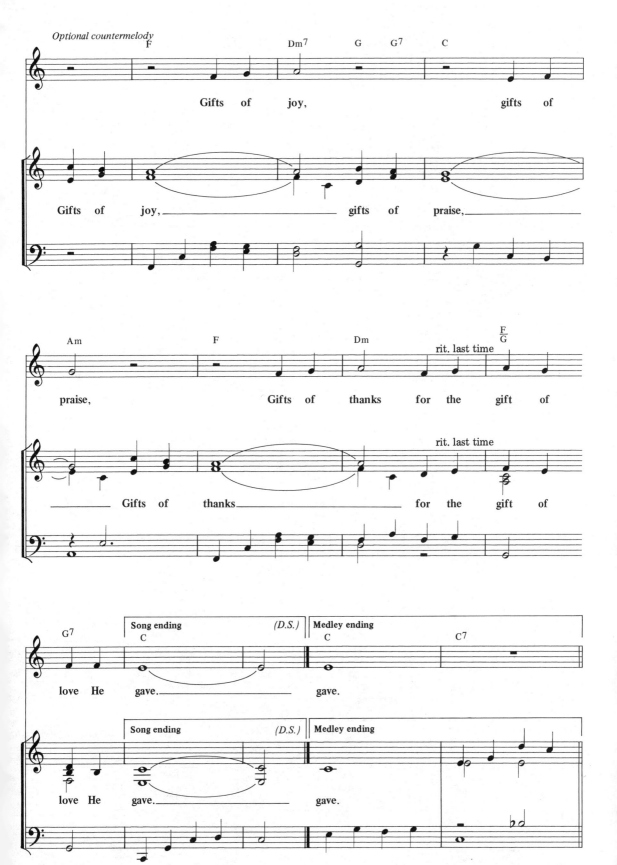

24 Jesus, I Love You

O. S.

(Ps. 116:1; 2 Cor. 5:14-15)

OTIS SKILLINGS
Arr. by Joseph Linn

25
Fill in the Blanks

(Dan. 6:16-22; Jon. 1:17; Luke 19:1-4)

D. R.

DOTTIE RAMBO and DAVE HUNTSINGER

1. Out in the sea, in the mid - dle of the
2. Up in a tree, in the top____ of a
3. Down in the den, in the bot - tom of the

deep ____ blue sea, A great____ big____ whale was____
syc - a - more tree, Sat a lit - tle man on a
li - ons' den, The king____ threw____ (whoop) to the

swim - min' by; And boy,____ was he in____ for a big sur - prise! He
limb so high. He heard ____ that ____ (whoop) would be pass - in' by. He
hun - gry beasts; The li - ons get - tin' read - y for a great big feast. They

26

A Psalm for Singing

(Ps. 95:1, 3)

Adapted by C. K.

CHARLES KIRBY

Show His Love Medley

Arr. by Joseph Linn

HEART TO CHANGE THE WORLD: vv. 1 & 2, coda. MY HANDS ARE THE HANDS: vv. 1 & 2, medley ending 2nd time.

27   Heart to Change the World

(Matt. 28:18-20; Rom. 10:13-15)

DEBBY RETTINO

D. R.

1. You and I've _____ got to have _____ a
2. Je-sus told _____ us to go _____ and

heart to change the world. _____ Let the song _____
share in ev-'ry land, _____ O-ver seas, _____

start to sing _____ in ev-'ry boy and girl. _____
through the hills, _____ a-cross the des-ert sand. _____

28 My Hands Are the Hands

(Rom. 6:13; 10:13-15; 2 Tim. 2:20-21)

D. R.

DEBBY RETTINO

1. My hands are the hands that God will use to show the world His love. When peo-ple look at me, they'll see a bit of heav'n a-bove.

2. My feet are the feet that God will use to car-ry forth the light. If

3. My voice is the voice that God will use to tell the world He cares, To

Praise Him Medley

Arr. by Joseph Linn

GIVE ME JOY IN MY HEART: vv. 1-3, with refrain; medley ending 3rd time. HALLELUJAH!: twice (2nd time slower), medley ending.

29   Give Me Joy in My Heart

(Mark 11:9-10; Gal. 5:22)

Traditional   Traditional
Arr. by Joseph Linn

1. Give me joy in my heart, keep me prais - ing. Give me joy in my heart, I pray. Give me joy in my heart, keep me prais-ing. Keep me prais-ing till the break of day.
2. Give me peace in my heart, keep me lov - ing. Give me peace in my heart, I pray. Give me peace in my heart, keep me lov-ing. Keep me lov-ing till the break of day.
3. Give me love in my heart, keep me serv - ing. Give me love in my heart, I pray. Give me love in my heart, keep me serv-ing. Keep me serv-ing till the break of day.

30

Hallelujah!

(Ps. 150:6)

Traditional

Traditional
Arr. by Joseph Linn

31 In My Father's House

Traditional

(John 14:1-3)

T.

Arr. by Josep..

*1. Come and go with me to my Fa-ther's house, to my Fa-ther's house,
2. It's not ver-y far to my Fa-ther's house, to my Fa-ther's house,
*3. Je-sus is the way to my Fa-ther's house, to my Fa-ther's house,

to my Fa-ther's house. Come and go with me to my Fa-ther's
to my Fa-ther's house. It's not ver-y far to my Fa-ther's
to my Fa-ther's house. Je-sus is the way to my Fa-ther's

house where there's joy, joy, joy.
house where there's joy, joy, joy.
house where there's joy, joy, joy.

joy, joy, joy, joy.

Optional verses:
4. Jesus is the Light in my Father's house . . .
5. All is peace and love in my Father's house . . .
6. We shall praise the Lord in my Father's house . . .

*Verses 1 & 3 on recording (with optional final ending).

Jesus Is a Gentleman

(Rev. 3:20)

K. H.

KATHIE HILL

Je - sus is a gen - tle - man who
Je - sus is a gen - tle - man who

nev - er forc - es His way in. He stands knock - ing
waits so pa - tient - ly and then He prays you will

at your door un - til you let Him in.
ask Him in to

33 Kids Under Construction
(Phil. 1:6)

GLORIA GAITHER and G. S. P.   WILLIAM J. GAITHER and GARY S. PAXTON

Kids un - der con - struc - tion;

May - be the paint is still wet.

Kids un - der con - struc - tion; The

*Verses 1 & 3 on recording.

34

Take a Step of Faith

(Ps. 18:28; 46:1-2; 2 Cor. 5:7; Heb. 11:8)

K. H.

KATHIE HILL

No mat-ter how tight the spot you're in, here's what you should do: Put your best foot for-ward and God will see you through.

Take a step of faith, take a step of

Resurrection Medley

Arr. by Joseph Linn

CHRIST IS RISEN TODAY: v. 1, medley ending. I LIVE: once, medley ending.

35 Christ Is Risen Today

CHARLES WESLEY and P. W.   (Matt. 28:6)   PAUL and DONNA WILLIAMS

1. Christ, the Lord, is ris-en to-day, Sons of men and an-gels say. Raise your joys and tri-umphs high; Sing,— heav-en and earth re-ply. Christ, the Lord, is ris-en to-day.

2. Praise the Lord of heav-en and earth. Praise the Lord who gave us worth. Al-le-lu-ia, let— us sing; Al-le-lu-ia, praise the King.

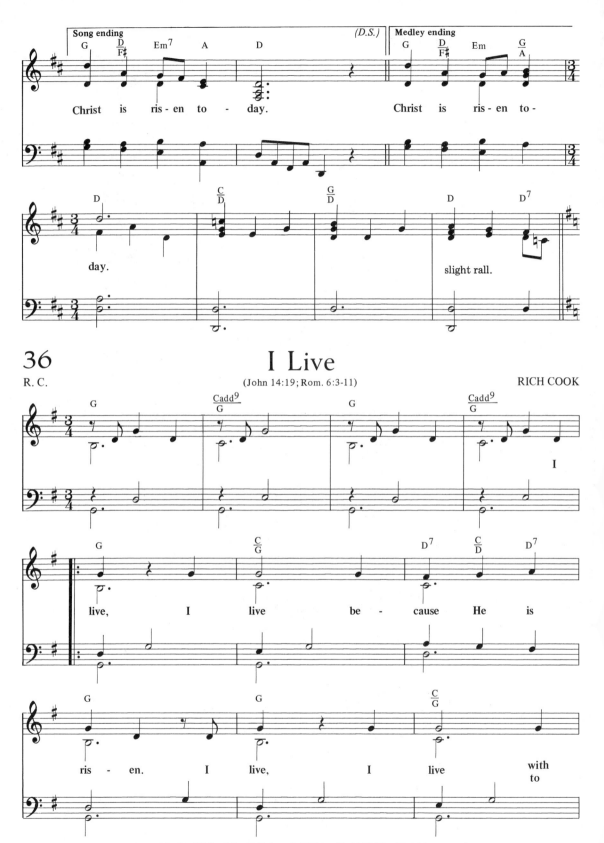

36 I Live

R. C.

(John 14:19; Rom. 6:3-11)

RICH COOK

Father Abraham
(Gal. 3:7, 29)

Traditional

Traditional
Arr. by Joseph Linn

With a shuffle

Fa-ther

Ab - ra - ham had man - y sons; Man - y sons had Fa - ther

Ab - ra - ham. I am one of them and so are you,

So let's just praise the Lord. ¹Right arm! Lord. Right

Left arm
Right Foot
Left Foot
Chin up
Turn around
Sit down

1. Right arm: move right arm back and forth like walking, with fist clenched and elbow bent. Do this motion while singing through the song again.
2. Left arm: add the left arm in the same manner as the right.
3. Right foot: add the right leg stepping up and down.
4. Left foot: add the left foot, so that you are walking in place.
5. Chin up: add chin moving up and down.
6. Turn around: turn in place while doing all the above.
7. Sit down: the end!

The Fruit of the Spirit Medley

Arr. by Joseph Linn

THE FRUIT OF THE SPIRIT: once. THE FRUIT SONG: vv. 1 & 2, medley ending 2nd time.

38   The Fruit of the Spirit

(Gal. 5:22)

P. J. and H. J.

PETER and HANNEKE JACOBS

Love, joy, peace,

Pa - tience, kind - ness, good-ness, faith, Gen - tle - ness and

self con-trol; This is the fruit of the Spir - it.

The Fruit Song

39

J. B.

(Gal. 5:22)

JOANNE BARRETT
Arr. by Joseph Linn

*Additional verses: peace, patience, kindness, goodness, faith, gentleness, self-control.

Big Things Medley

Arr. by Joseph Linn

BIG THINGS: vv. 1 & 3, medley ending 2nd time. IT'S THE LITTLE THINGS: vv. 1 & 2.

40   Big Things

C. G.

(John 6:1-13; Rom. 6:13)

CAROL GADDY
Arr. by Joseph Linn

ti - ny lunch He blessed the bread and fed the mul - ti - tudes; And He'll use us, too, when we

give our - selves to Him.

2. You
3. ʔ

Him.

3 Medley ending

Him,

to Him._____

41   It's the Little Things

B. B.

(Matt. 10:40-42; 25:40)

BOYD BACON
Arr. by Joseph Linn

1. It's the lit - tle things that show our love for Je - sus. It's the
2. It's the lit - tle things we do each day for oth - ers. It's the

The Peace Love Joy Medley

Arr. by Joseph Linn

I'VE GOT PEACE LIKE A RIVER: vv. 1-3, medley ending 3rd time. DOWN IN MY HEART: vv. 1-3, medley ending 3rd time.

42 I've Got Peace Like a River

(Isa. 48:18)

Spiritual

Spiritual
Arr. by Joseph Linn

1. I've got peace like a river, I've got peace like a river, I've got
2. I've got love like an ocean, I've got love like an ocean, I've got
3. I've got joy like a fountain, I've got joy like a fountain, I've got

43   Down in My Heart

G. W. C.   (Gal. 5:22; Phil. 4:7)   GEORGE W. COOKE
Arr. by Joseph Linn

1. I have the
2. I have the
3. I have the

joy,—— joy,—— joy,—— joy——
peace that pass - eth un - der - stand - ing down in my heart,
love of Je - sus, love of Je - sus

down in my heart, down in my heart. I have the

I have the
I have the
I have the

Christmas Medley

Arr. by Joseph Linn

BETHLEHEM LULLABY: vv. 1 & 2, medley ending 2nd time. CHRISTMAS IS A TIME TO LOVE: once, medley ending.

44 Bethlehem Lullaby

(Luke 2:1-14)

P. W. BLACKMER

Adapted from Brahms
Arr. by Joseph Linn

1. Long a - go there was born, in the cit - y of David, A_____ sweet, ho - ly_____ Babe who was Je - sus, our King. An - gels sang at His birth, "Lul-la-
2. Je - sus came as a child from His Fa - ther in heav - en, And has shown us the_____ way to be lov - ing and kind. While the stars sang a - bove, "Lul-la-

by, peace on earth." An-gels sang at His birth, "Lul-la-
by, God is love." While the stars sang a-bove, "Lul-la-

Song ending *(D.S.)*

Medley ending

by,___ peace on earth."
by,___ God is love." love."

45 Christmas Is a Time to Love

E. R. and D. R. (1 John 4:9-11) ERNIE and DEBBIE RETTINO

Christ-mas is a time,

Christ-mas is a time, Christ-mas is a time to love.___ love. We

of-ten start to wor-ry, and peo-ple get up-set If things don't all go right on Christmas

46 Joyful, Joyful, We Adore You

LINDA LEE JOHNSON (Ps. 19:1; Luke 2:8-20; 2 Cor. 9:15) From Ludwig von Beethoven
Arr. by Joseph Linn

1. Joy-ful, joy - ful, we a - dore You, God of glo - ry, Lord of light;
2. All your works de - clare Your glo - ry; All cre - a - tion joins to sing.

An - gels lift - ing praise be - fore You Sing through-out this ho - ly night.
Praise re - sounds as earth re - joic - es In the birth of Christ, the King.

In a man-ger lies a — ba - by, Child of — Ma - ry, Son of God. Voic - es
Shep-herds kneel be - fore the — In - fant; Trum-pets sound and an - thems raise, As with

joined in joy - ful cho - rus Praise You for Your gift of love.
joy our hearts are lift - ed, Joined in won - der, love, and praise.

47 Praise to the Infant King

(Luke 2:8-20)

NAN ALLEN

DENNIS ALLEN
Arr. by Joseph Linn

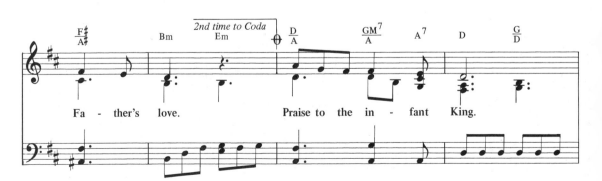

48 Christmas Isn't Christmas
(Till It Happens in Your Heart)
(Rev. 3:20)

C. O.

JIMMY and CAROL OWENS

Christ - mas is -n't Christ - mas till it hap - pens in your heart; Some - where deep in - side you is where Christ - mas real - ly starts. So give your heart to

2nd time to Coda

Je - sus; you'll dis - cov - er when you do That it's

Christ - mas, real - ly Christ - mas for you.

Je - sus brings warmth like a win - ter fire, A light like a can - dle's

glow. He's wait - ing now to come in - side As He

did so long a - go. Je - sus brings gifts of

49

K-K-Kazoo

(Ps. 47:1; 149:1; 150:4)

R. S.

RANDY SHARPE

Moderate ♩ = 118

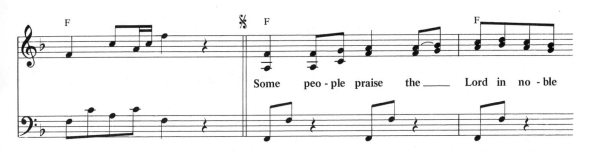

Some peo - ple praise the ___ Lord in no - ble

song, Dig - ni - fied and strong, robes that are too long.

In high-est maj - es - ty our God a - dored. But there's an-oth-er way to praise the

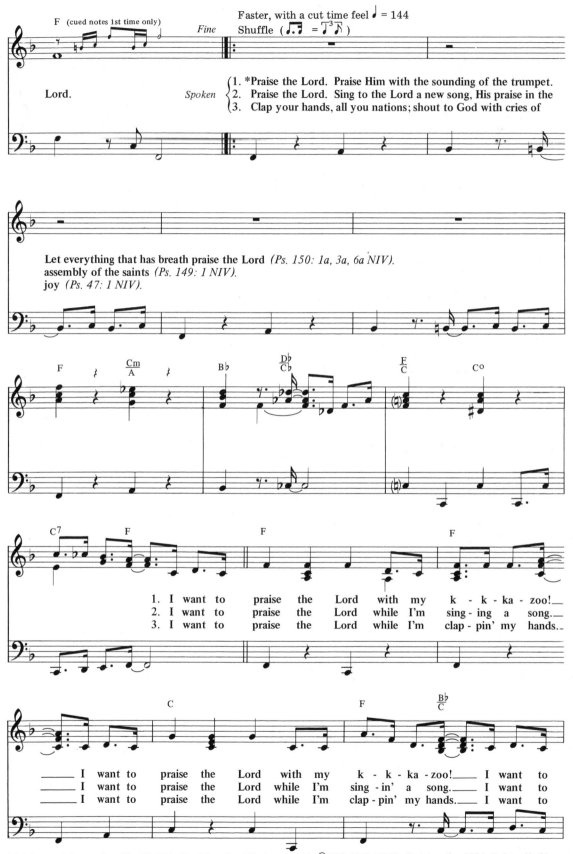

Faster, with a cut time feel ♩ = 144
Shuffle

F (cued notes 1st time only)   *Fine*

Lord.   *Spoken*
1. *Praise the Lord. Praise Him with the sounding of the trumpet.
2. Praise the Lord. Sing to the Lord a new song, His praise in the
3. Clap your hands, all you nations; shout to God with cries of

Let everything that has breath praise the Lord *(Ps. 150: 1a, 3a, 6a NIV)*.
assembly of the saints *(Ps. 149: 1 NIV)*.
joy *(Ps. 47: 1 NIV)*.

1. I want to praise the Lord with my k - k - ka - zoo!___
2. I want to praise the Lord while I'm sing - ing a song.___
3. I want to praise the Lord while I'm clap - pin' my hands.___

_____ I want to praise the Lord with my k - k - ka - zoo!___ I want to
_____ I want to praise the Lord while I'm sing - in' a song.___ I want to
_____ I want to praise the Lord while I'm clap - pin' my hands.___ I want to

*Scripture quotations are from *The Holy Bible, New International Version,* copyright ©1973, 1978, 1984 by the International Bible Society. Used by permission.

praise the Lord with my k-k-ka-zoo!
praise the Lord while I'm sing-in' a song.
praise the Lord while I'm clap-pin' my hands.

K-k-k-k-
S-s-s-s-
K-k-k-k-

k-k-k-k- k-k-ka-zoo.
s-s-s-s- sing-in' a song.
k-k-k-k- clap-pin' my hands.

(Play mel. on kazoos)
(Sing "la, la, la," etc.)
(Clap rhythm of mel.)

(Back to Tempo I on D.S.)

D.S. al Fine

50

That's Good!

(Gen. 1)

D. A. and N. A.

DENNIS and NAN ALLEN

Shuffle

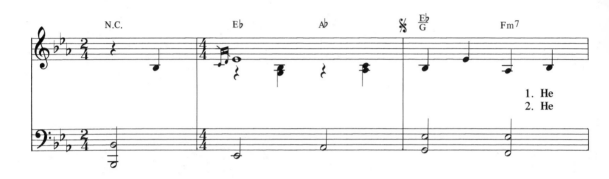

1. He
2. He

made the wa - ter wet, He made the land __ stay dry. He put twin-kle in the stars and __
put a touch of wag __ in a pup-py dog's tail, __ Then put a lit - tle slow in a

blue __ in the sky. And when He was sure it worked as it should, God
sil - ly old __ snail.

ALPHABETICAL INDEX
Song and *Medley* Titles